Raising Baby

Fawns Become Family

by

Jim MacLachlan

Photographs by Eilene Poole

Copyright 2021

Raising wild animals at home is illegal in many areas for a lot of good reasons, so don't try this at home. The instincts that keep them alive in their natural habitat can be deadly in a domestic situation. Saving a wild animal & releasing it back into the wild requires an intimate knowledge of that particular species, its habits, & the area. Any professional will tell you plenty of tragic stories. The very act of raising a wild animal negates their fear of humans &, if they are a prey animal such as a deer, makes them an easy target for hunters. They can also become an intolerable pest as the tragic story of "The Yearling" describes.

A deer seems like a beautiful, harmless animal, but their speed & power are incredible. Their hooves are sharp & deadly. Almost every year I read about a hunter being injured or even killed when their wounded quarry suddenly lashes out. This happens whenever the deer is startled. They don't think, just react.

Buddy was standing on the back porch while I fed biscuits to him & the dogs. Just as he was about to take it, for no apparent reason, he suddenly leaped to the side & landed in the yard about where I'm standing on the far left in the picture above. That sideways jump took him eight feet to the side, over the three foot railing, & yet below the beam which is only about six feet up. He did it so quickly that I just stood there & blinked. I had trouble believing my eyes. He was suddenly standing perfectly relaxed facing in the same direction, but eight feet to the side. Anyone in the way of his 125 hurtling pounds would have been badly injured, though.

When an animal reaches puberty, their personality changes & they can become dangerous. Playful, friendly raccoon babies suddenly become vicious & frantic to escape enclosures where they've been content for almost a year. Domestic livestock such as bulls, stallions, rams, & buck goats that are hand-raised will often see humans as possible competitors or breeding partners which can lead to deadly, tragic accidents that often result in the death of the animal.

Today there are a lot of facilities to help the public with wild animals. If you find one that you think needs rescuing, search the Internet for a wildlife rehab services or center nearby. Call them & discuss the situation. **Most of the time, keeping your distance is by far the best thing you can do both for yourself & the animal.** Observe them briefly & do NOT touch! You may be condemning a helpless baby to a horrible death simply because the presence or smell of a human will scare off the mother.

This book has hyperlinks to outside sites & articles. They'll amplify my explanations. I tried to only use stable, safe sites, but click on them at your own risk. Things change rapidly on the Internet & are beyond my control.

Table of Contents

Introduction:

Dead deer are an all too common sight on the sides of roads. A startled deer reacts quickly, but the reflexes & instincts which served them well for thousands of years don't work well with cars. They don't seem to understand just how fast & dangerous they are. The death of a doe can leave an orphaned fawn hidden nearby. Very young ones may starve to death &/or make a meal for a scavenger or predator. If they do wander into sight, they're often hit by another car, but occasionally one defies the odds & survives to be rescued.

North-central Maryland in the 1990s was a rural area filled with white-tailed deer. While an orphaned fawn was a sad sight, there weren't any public facilities around for taking care of the situation, so we usually let nature take its course. The times & area were changing, though. Farmers were selling off their land to developers & suburbia was springing up. Some of the hardships we took for granted were unacceptable to our new neighbors & one couple decided my mother could save a fawn they found. They were right & she went on to raise quite a few. These are their stories…

Baby

Driving home one afternoon day in June 1992, a new neighbor saw a day-old fawn standing next to its dead mother on the side of the road. The woman knew my mother had a flock of sheep & a lot of other animals, so she put the fawn in her car & took it to Mom hoping she could help.

Mom had the facilities. Her farm took up most of a small valley created by Deer Creek where she raised Bantam chickens, Cornish Game hens, Guineas, peacocks, & other fowl. She also fed semi wild ducks & geese on the several ponds. A variety of livestock dotted the fields, but the money makers were the flock fifty Dorset sheep & a dozen Angus steers.

Dorset sheep wool is rather coarse & doesn't sell for much, so they were primarily raised for their meat. The lambs were an Easter specialty with people coming from miles around to buy directly. Her fifty ewes usually had over 100 lambs each year since quite a few had three lambs each. Sometimes a ewe died or didn't produce enough milk, so Mom had a backup stock for emergencies. It turned out that her feed stock & knowledge worked just as well on fawns as it did on lambs.

Baby is about two months old in the picture above. Even though she was perfectly safe on the farm, her natural instincts were to find a hidden, secluded place to nap.

Hand-raising a fawn or any young mammal isn't easy. Not only do they need frequent feeding throughout the day & night at first, but their diet is somewhat specialized. For the first few days, the mother produces 'early milk' or colostrum which is very thick & filled with extra calories, bacteria, antibodies, & other good things to help the newborn. It wasn't available commercially back then, but Mom milked some from ewes that produced really well & stored it in the freezer. That meant Baby had a better start in life than most orphaned deer at the time.

After a few days, the mother's milk thins into the common sort & that is commercially available. My Aunt Janet is feeding Baby of the human baby food Pablum™ mixed with powdered calf replacer milk from a bottle that would normally feed a lamb or calf.

When Baby was about a month old, she gave up the bottle & started eating from a bowl four times a day. Baby needed less of the baby food as she ate more vegetation on her own, so she was cut back to three times a day when she was two months old. At three & a half months, she was only getting fed twice a day.

Mom's German Shepard bitch, Fern, is cleaning her bottom at the same time, a chore she liked quite a lot. It stimulated Baby to poop which was important for her health & Fern liked to eat the produce. Mom always had at least a few dogs around the farm to keep predators away. For decades, they had been mutts, but those could vary too much in personality & abilities. She wanted a breed that was better suited to protecting her sheep & other livestock. Fern did a great job at that & also assumed a new role as surrogate mother to the fawns.

Baby thought of Fern as her mother, so she tried to get a meal, but didn't have any luck. Occasionally consistent nursing can cause a bitch to give milk, but none of the fawns managed to get it out of Fern.

Baby is trying for another meal while out in the field.

Fern cleaned Baby all over. Here she's getting her face washed. It doesn't look as if she likes it much more than my kids did.

Baby followed Fern who followed Mom, so she wandered all around the farm & that included one of the ponds where Mom fed the wild ducks & geese once or twice a day.

Ducks & geese like to browse the banks of ponds for grass, bugs, & gravel which they store in their gizzard to help them digest their food. Unfortunately, that erodes the banks & causes ponds to silt in much faster. When we dug the pond, its sides angled evenly down to & below the water, but here you can see Baby walking on a shelf where the bank has been eaten away.

As she grew, Baby ventured further into the pond. She was the only deer who ever swam with the dogs. None of the others liked the water as much. She wouldn't play with my kids the way the dogs did, but she certainly had no fear of my youngest boy, Brandon.

Mom is showing off the tennis ball before throwing it into the pond. Pete & Jack are the two Labrador Retrievers. Baby looks just as interested as the dogs.

Baby couldn't open her mouth wide enough to get a grip on the ball, though.

Even though she couldn't fetch the ball herself, Baby had fun following the dogs into the pond as they swam out & retrieved it. Baby still has all her spots, so she's less than three months old.

Sometimes Fern got the ball & this time Baby decided to swim off on her own.

Fern is telling Baby that the tennis ball is hers, but it's just play.

As Baby grew, she lost her spots & became more adventurous. In this picture, she is about three & half months old & is exploring the edge of the creek. Deer Creek ran through the center of the farm with about half in the backwaters of the Eden Mill Dam, an old flour mill that is now part of a park. It's about a mile downstream from the farm.

In the coldest winters, we could ice skate on the creek from below the house all the way down to the dam. During the summers, we often swam, canoed, & kayaked to it & back since there wasn't much current in the backwater. The dam was refaced when I was a teenager, so we used to slide down it. I tried that about 15 years later, but it wasn't any fun since the dam face had roughened. The fast, one-way trip down the face of the dam wore the seat out of my shorts & the skin off the palms of my hands as I alternated which body part I was going to sand away. Ouch! Now that it's a state park, they don't allow such antics.

Baby is curiously eyeing the cat sitting in the basement way of the house as she walks up the front lawn. Behind her you can see the pond with the creek & the meadow beyond. The tan spots in the meadow are rolls of hay about five feet in diameter that were recently baled.

Mom has Baby eating out of her hand.

Baby was allowed to wander where she would as were the dogs since the house was about a quarter mile from the road via the lane. While it was only about two hundred yards to the road through the fields on the right, they were steep so the animals didn't wander up that way very often unless we did, too.

Baby grew as the year wore on. The picture above was taken in the fall. Pete is on the left then Baby, Fern, & Jack is on the far right. As usual, Jack has a tennis ball in her mouth & you can see the pink ribbon Mom put on Baby in an attempt to keep her safe from hunters.

It was a tough decision whether or not to put a ribbon on Baby. No one should have been hunting on the farm, but Baby was starting to wander further. She had no fear of humans, so Mom's hope was that any hunter who saw her would realize she was special for some reason & leave her alone.

Mom is scratching Baby's head while my youngest two watch. Her husband, Rip, is on the porch directly behind Baby.

Erin didn't appreciate Baby nipping her on the cheek. Wild animals rarely socialize perfectly.

Baby's coat was quite thick as you can by the way the snow just piled on her without melting.

Baby helped with the sheep, too.

A bunch of us are chatting on the back porch at Christmas while Mom fed Baby a treat & peacock looked in the window at the festivities.

Baby stood for a treat from Mom on January 8, 1993 while Jack sniffed next to them. This is the last picture of Baby since she wandered off later that day & never returned. That was hard, but not unexpected since she was now seven months old & wanted the company of her own kind. Even a hand-raised deer is only tamed until their hormones kick in. As a doe, she had a pretty good chance of surviving. Doe hunting seasons were short to nonexistent in Maryland at the time, so she should have been safe from hunters.

Buddy

The second fawn Mom fostered was Buddy who showed up one dark & stormy June night in 1993 when a couple found him standing next to his dead mother on the side of the road.

He is two weeks old in these pictures which were taken in July 1993.

He was about 7 weeks old in these pictures from August 1993 as he gets a drink from the pond & kisses Fern.

He's giving Fern more kisses & playing with Jack below.

Buddy was never housebroken, but he did wander into the mud room occasionally. He's about 8 weeks old at the end of August 1993. While deer urine is quite rank, they don't pee nearly as often as they poop & the latter are rather dry, hard pellets that are easily cleaned up.

Buddy is inspecting some leaves from a plant of Mom's, but not eating them. He was very good about not eating things that were bad for him.

Chick inspection & something of interest is lurking in the garden.

In the beginning of November 1993, Buddy still had a few spots left, but they were gone by the end of the month when he was 5 months old.

Buddy didn't like walking in the upper pond next to the house since the mud was too deep.

A Bantam rooster watches Mom feed banana slices, skin & all, to Buddy.

It's Fern's turn to get her face washed.

It was a warm day in December 1993 when my kids, Brandon, James, & Erin, posed for this picture with Buddy.

Buddy was raised with all kinds of critters. My daughter with her dangling mittens probably seems stranger to him than the Guinea Hens in the next picture.

Merry Christmas! With the way his tongue is sticking out, I don't think Buddy thought much of the gifts under the tree.

Nope, he wasn't impressed at all.

January 1994 got cold & white, but it didn't bother Buddy. His coat was amazingly thick. Still, why walk when you can ride?

Buddy looks very much at home in the woods.

He was equally at ease standing on this tin roof in the snow, though. He was very adaptable.

In April 1994, his coat isn't as pretty since he's shedding out all the winter hair he no longer needs.

Mom put out some feed for the white peacock, but Buddy got it first.

In May 1994, Buddy decided Pete needed her eyes cleaned.

In July 1994, Buddy was a year old & he shed his first full coat.

Buddy could really run fast when he wanted to.

He was allowed to attend this outdoor party in August 1994. As you can see, the crowd didn't bother him at all. He could have been anywhere on the farm, but instead he was mooching at the table. Mom obviously spoiled him since she wouldn't let her dogs do that.

These photos
were taken by
Billy's human.

Billy the deer:

His Mother is a German Shepherd

leftover Christmas lawn ornament, the driver stopped. The situation was immediately apparent. The stranger, knowing by Billy's yet unfolded ears that he couldn't be more than a day old, also knew that he must act fast or the fawn would surely perish.

So, in the pouring rain, in an act of uncommon kindness, the stranger picked up the shivering fawn, who offered little resistance, and took him to a farm where there might be some hope, however slim.

Upon the arrival of this pair, the owner of the farm, in another act of uncommon kindness, sprung into action. She also knew that if the fawn was to be saved it would have to be done in haste. She would need milk, which could easily be obtained from the farm's goat, and warmth through the damp night. But how to keep this baby warm was going to be a problem. Or was it?

Fay, Oscar and Billy head for shore after chasing the ball into the pond

She walked right past the pondering pair and carefully nestled her warm, furry body around the young infant without so much as a sound. Although slightly in shock at what had just happened, the two ponderers decided not to today, nearly a year later, Billy thinks and acts more like a dog than a deer. It also explains why he nearly ran me over upon my arrival and his affinity for milk bones.

The bond between dog and deer may at first seem un- farm where it's safe. But I can't force him to. He's free to come and go as he pleases and that's the way it should be. As a afterthought she adds, almost wishfully, " Maybe I'll put a fluorescent collar on him so that a hunter will have on his own. To think of Billy getting shot after all of this is to sad to contemplate. This is not a indictment against hunters, who have their place. But if you are a hunter and happen to come across a buck who's wearing a fluorescent

Buddy gained a bit of fame when Steve Collison wrote an article about him for the local newspaper, The North County News. You'll notice his name is Billy in the article. The picture lists Fay & Oscar swimming with him, but it's obviously Fern & Jack & the picture is that of Baby, not Buddy. I'm not sure if Steve changed his name & some of the details to protect Mom's anonymity, but some was obviously for dramatic effect. It was a very well written & moving piece, if not entirely accurate.

 Buddy was a little over a year old in September 1994, just before hunting season. He had no fear of humans so would have been easy prey for any hunter if he wandered too far from home. Not wanting him to die young, Mom castrated him which kept him close to home. It also kept him from getting a set of antlers which would attract hunters & be a danger to the dogs & humans. In the picture above, you can see his horn buds formed, but they never got any bigger after he was cut.

Buddy had a great life with complete freedom of the farm. He couldn't be any more relaxed in the picture below. This was taken on a warm day in December 1994.

In October 1995, Buddy is curled up with Pete ready to take a ride in Mom's van. She was probably just carrying some supplies down to one of the barns. Buddy could have run there faster, but he thinks he's just one of the dogs.

This is the last picture we have of Buddy. Hunting season started not long after this was taken & he just wasn't around anymore. It was a very sad time. We guessed that he strayed too near the road. Well, he had a good 2-1/2 years of life, about average for a wild white-tailed deer. (Like their cousin, the goat, they can live to about twenty years old, but they rarely live longer than a decade in the wild.) That was far longer & better than if he'd been left by the side of the road that rainy night.

Other Fawns

Mom never actively sought fawns to foster, but they trickled in throughout the decade. Fern patiently puts up with a fawn's inspection.

Mom raised some additional German Shepard bitches who all took their fawn raising duties seriously. Brooke & Hope are carefully inspecting this fawn & will lick it clean from stem to stern.

Pete, a Labrador bitch, was nice enough to the fawns, but not really interested in them beyond an occasional sniff. As you can see, Fern is watching their interaction closely. She was quite protective of her fawns.

This month-old German Shepard puppy wants to play with a fawn inspecting one of the puppy toys.

This trio looks like trouble.

Sometimes the attention from the dogs could get a little overwhelming.

Bantam cocks are fairly small birds, but not much smaller than this fawn.

This fawn looks as if it is in a rush to get out of its hiding place in the flower bed. It's probably time to get fed or go for a walk.

This fawn is licking the ear of Toby, my Aunt Janet's Jack Russell Terrier. Toby starred in dozens of TV commercials in his younger days. He's most famous for running on top of a Goodyear tire.

The fawns weren't choosey about who fed them or where they were as Marilyn, a friend of my mother's, is demonstrating.

Once Mom raised a set of twins.

Kate was their protector & surrogate mother.

Afterword:

Before digital photos became common place, we took far fewer & the quality was always a crap shoot. Back in the 1990s, Mom had a Kodak Pocket Instamatic 110 camera that used film which came in cartridges. She usually kept a cartridge that took 24 color pictures in the camera & bought a new one when she dropped off the used one for processing at the local pharmacy. It might take months or even a year to use up the roll of film & then it took a week to get the pictures back. In other words, it was a fairly expensive & drawn out process that wasn't high on the priority list.

All the pictures in this book were taken with Mom's camera, mostly by her. When she's in the picture, the photographer was whoever was handy. She took pictures only when she thought of it & most weren't good enough to make it into her photo album. A couple of decades later, I pulled those out & scanned them all. Several more years went by before I attempted to put them all together into this book, so that explains the varying quality of the pictures. I'm sure a professional could have touched them up, but I decided that it was better just to see them as they are.

It was neat having fawns around & a great experience for my kids, but it was a lot of work & heartbreak for Mom. She'd spend all that time caring for them, nursing them into fine specimens, only to have them wander off forever usually in less than a year later to unknown fates. Buddy was especially difficult since there was only one reason we could think of for his disappearance. It's likely some hunter shot him most unfairly. He probably had a pink ribbon around his neck, although that wasn't certain. It attached by Velcro so it could tear loose if he got it hung up on something. We looked, but never found it, so we doubt that was the case.

If you liked this book, a review is always appreciated since each makes a huge difference in sales. More of my books are available on Smashwords.com & Amazon. For my books describing construction procedures, I recommend buying them from Smashwords where multiple formats are available including a PDF which is easy to print out for use in the shop.

If you want to get in touch, just look me up on Goodreads.com where I moderate the "General Craft & DIY" as well as the "Evolution of Science Fiction" groups. Registration is free & they don't send spam. It's a great place to discuss books or most anything else.